MIDNIGHT GLITTERS

SHINE IN DARK

ISHA KHANDELWAL

Copyright © Isha Khandelwal
All Rights Reserved.

To my parents ofcourse, my sister and brother. my friends who always supported me and especially to my imaginary love without whom my overthinking mind couldn't think of it.

Contents

Preface	*vii*
1. Chapter 1	1
2. Chapter 2	3
3. Chapter 3	5
4. Chapter 4	7
5. Chapter 5	9
6. Chapter 6	11
7. Chapter 7	13
8. Chapter 8	15
9. Chapter 9	17
10. Chapter 10	20

Preface

"THERE IS A LIGHT AT THE END OF EVERY TUNNEL".

THIS IS THAT ONE QUOTE WHICH ALWAYS KEEPS ME MOTIVATED. SO, I TARTED WRITING POETRY IN 2020,THE LOCKDOWN PHASE. I WAS A CAREFREE GIRL WHO TURNED INTO AN OVERTHINKER. AND HERE I AM WRITING THIS BOOK BY MAKING MY WEAKNESS AS MY STRENGHT. THE SCENARIOS CREATED IN MY MIND FOR ANY SITUATIO IF THIS HAPPENS AND ALL SO WHY NOT TO WRITE IT DOWN IN THIS WAY? YA,SOME OF INCIDENTS ARE TRUE.SHHHH SECRET!!

ANWAYS, THIS IS MY VERY OWN FIRST BOOK. I KNOW THERE MIGHT BE MANY MISTAKES IN THIS BUT PRACTICE MAKES A MAN PERFECT. LOVE TO EACH ONE OF YOU WHO ARE READING THIS.

LOVE,LOST,HOPE,HEAL.

Chapter1

HER FIERY EYES SPEAKS EVERYTHING SHE HIDES
THE BEAUTIFUL SMILE SHE CARRIES
DEPICTS THE DEEPEST TERRIFYING SUFFERINGS.
HER ACTION SHOWS HOW KEEN SHE IS
GER HEART IS CRYING, GO GIVE HER SOME LOVE
GO AND FLY ON THE WALL AND BELL THE CAT
FOR WHAT ALL SHE NEEDS.
FOR SHE IS A PAXISTIMA
TAKE HER TO THE MOUNTAIN.
SEE THE SUN KISSING HER FACE,
AND WIND TOUCHING HER BODY
THE BIRDS SINGING FOR HER,
AND TREES BEING HER LOVE.
GO AND SEE HOW HAPPY SHE IS WITH THESE THINGS
GO AND SEE THE REAL SHE WHO IS NOW WRAPPED WITH LOVE AND HAPPINESS.
GO AND SAY HER EVERYTHING
GO AND LISTEN TO HER EVERY NEED.
YOU CAN'T FIND HER IN CROUDS
FOR SHE LOVES PEACE
YOU CAN'T KNOW HER, UNTILL SHE WISH.

LIKE SUNFLOWERS WHICH NO MATTER WHAT
DIRECTION THEY ARE PLANTED,
TURN TOWARDS THE SUN
SHE TOO EGANTURNING IN THE DIRECTION
THAT NOURISHED HER.
SHE IS SCARED OF NOT KNOWING WHAT WILL
COME NEXT
AS NO ONE REALLY KNOWS WHAT THE SURPRISE
IS GOING TO .
SO WHAT IF THE SURPRISE ISN'T WHAT SHE IS
EXPECTING?
AND IS MESSES UP HER ENTIRE LIFE.
SHE OFTEN FOUND HERSELF DRIFTING AWAY
FROM REALITY.
SEEKING SANTUARY WITHIN A WORLD FULL OF
IMPOSSIBLE DAYDREAMS.
SEE,SHE IS STILL STANDING THERE
IN THE MOUNTAIN PEAK
GO HOLD HER HAND AND
MAKE FULFILL HER DREAMS.
SEE,SHE IS WAITING FOR
THE ENDLESS LOVE AND CARE
SEE,SHE IS TIRED OF EVERYTHING SHE BEAR.
~ISHA KHANDELWAL.

Chapter2

I AM CALM BUT NOT MY HEART AND MIND
SO MANY THINGS RUNS AT A TIME.
AMONG SO MANY REASONS ONE IS YOU,
WHO ROAM IN MY MIND DAY AND NIGHT.
I STARE AT THE SKY AND IT MAKES ME THINK OF YOU
OF HOW FAR YOU ARE YET I HAVE MY ARMS WRAPPED AROUND YOU
3AM AND I AM IN MY BALCONY,STILL WAITING FOR YOU
RAISING MY CUP OF TEA AS A TOAST TO YOU.
RAIN STARTS AND I HUG MY KNEES
LISTENING TO MUSIC WHICH AGAIN REMINDS ME OF YOU.
YOUR VOICE FOR WHICH I FALL
I WANT TO TALK TO SOMEONE AND THAT IS YOU.
I AM HYSTERICAL,FULL OF EMOTIONS
AND THUNDER BEGINS,AND YES, AGAIN A REMINDER
THIS TIME ITS NOT YOU , IT'S ME ,MY HEART AND MIND FIGHTING
FOR THE LOVE I HAVE FOR YOU AND HATE...

MY MOUTH IS SHUT BUT NOT MY MIND AND HEART

I AM FILLED INSIDE AND CALM OUTSIDE.

RAIN STOPS,SKY TURNED DARK,SUN DIDN'T RISE AND I AM LOST

LOST IN THE HOPE FOR YOU

LOST IN SEARCH FOR YOU

LOST IN SEEING US TOGETHER

IN MY WORLD,WHICH IS NOT EVEN POSSIBLE.

~ISHA KHANDELWAL

Chapter3

I LOVE BALTER PIROUTEE ALONE UNDER THE MOONLIGHT
FOR THE MOONLIGHT GIVES ME KICK
AND I FEEL LOVE BENETH THE BLANQUET OF STARS.
ME,IN A TRADITIONAL BLACK KURTI
OPEN HAIRS WITH A SMALL BINDI
COOL WINDS BLOWING AND SITTING IN DARKNESS
AS IF I AM EGARLY WAITING FOR THE MOON
TO SHOWER ITS LIGHT AND GIVES ME A HUG TIGHT.
"YOU ARE BEAUTIFUL AND BOLD ENOUGH" SAID THE MOON
I SMILED AND ASKED HIM FOR SOME LOVE AND SUPPORT
"WHENEVER YOU FEELS THAT YOUR HEART IS HEAVY,
JUST LOOK AT ME" SAID THE MOON.
I GAVE A SMILE AND THE MOON DISAPPEARED.
THE DAY, I CAME TO KNOW THE POWER OF LOVE
THE POWER OF BEING LOVEED.
I AM SO LOST IN MY THOUGHTS

THAT FOR A MOMENT I FORGOT EVERYTHING
AND I DIDN'T REALISED THAT THE NIGHT
PASSED
OH!MY HAPPY HOUR AND HAPPY PLACE
WILL SEE YOU AGAIN WHEN THE DAY PASS AWAY.
SOMEONE ONCE SAID, THAT BUTTERFLY IN
ONE'S STOMACH
GIVES THE HINT OF LOVE
AND NOW I CAN FEEL THAT LOVE.
THE ONLY THING ANONYMOUS TO ME IS
FOR WHOM IS THIS LOVE?
IS IT FOR THE MOON OR SOMEONE GOING TO BE
MY MOON?
-ISHA KHANDELWAL

Chapter4

GAZING AT THE MOON I WANDER
SOMETIMES WE DON'T NEED A HUMAN FOR CONVERSATION.
I LOOKED AR THE MOON FOR LONG ENOUGH TODAY
TO SEE HOW MOON SHINES EVEN IN HIS LONELINESS.
THE STARS WHICH ARE DISAPPEARED AND LEFT THE SKY INCOMPLETE
STILL THE MOON NEVER FAILS TO GIVE ME A SMILE.
STARS WERE LIKE THE BLANQUET TO THE SKY
NOW,THAT SPECTACULAR VIEW IS LEFT IN MY EYE.
HOW BEAUTIFUL OUR NATURE IS,AND SO IT GLOWS IN NIGHT
BUT EVERYTHING IS DESTROYED BY WE HUMANS OVERNIGHT.
HOW HARSH WE HUMAN CAN BE?
WE ALREADY DESTROYED THE TRUE BEAUTY.
IT FEELS LIKE I LOST THE SIGHT OF WHO I WAS
EVERYDAY, I COME UP TO THE SAME CONCLUSION

HEY, LOOK AT THE MOON!

WITHOUT STARS ALSO, IT COME UP WITH BEAUTIFUL ILLUSION

I AM NEVER ALONE, I AM THE WOLF HOWLING TO THE SAME MOON.

THE SOOTHING BREEZE,THE BEAUTIFUL MOON AND STARS SHINING IN MY EYES!

AHH! WHAT A PERFECT TRIO.

~ISHA KHANDELWAL

Chapter5

THE YELLOW DUSTY WEATHER,THE WARM WINDS BLOWING

ARE THEY THE INDICATION OF SOMETHING UNWANTED GOING?

THE SLIGHT RAIN AND THUNDERSTORM STARTED

SEEING THI I AM A LITTLE DISHEARTENED.

THE EMPTY ROAD AND DARK CLOUDS COVERING THE SKY

I DON'T KNOW WHY BUT ITS FRIGHTNING ME FROM INSIDE

THE INCREASING VOICE OF RAIN AND RAPID THUNDERSTORM,

DO THE NATURE GOD WANTS ME SOMETHING TO INFORM?

THE SKY LOOKS MURKY AND DULL

IT'S A LONELY KIND OF DAY

I WISH I WAS SEATED IN A MOUNTAIN

HEARING AN ORCHESTRA PLAY.

BE CALM MY HEART;AND ENJOY SINGING

BEHIND THE CLOUDS IS THE SUN STILL SHINING

SOME DAYS MUST BE DARK AND DREARY

BELIEVE ME, YOUR LIFE IS A BEAUTIFUL STORY.

~ISHA KHANDELWAL.
BELIEVE ME, YOUR

Chapter6

WHEN THE NIGHT IS FULL OF DARKNESS,
AND THE STARS IS DECORATED WITH SHIMMERING STARS
THE WIND BLOWS AND ITS SOOTHING TOUCH FEELS LIKE YOURS
A PURE SILENCE IN MY SIDE WITH A BUNCH OF QUESTIONS IN MY MIND
AND YOU ARE MISSED SO MUCH TONIGHT.
THE BLOWING WIND,THE SILENCE AND THE STARS REMIND ME OF YOURS
THROUGH THIS WIND I CAN FEEL YOUR TOUCH;
THROUGH THIS SILENCE I CAN FEEL THAT PEACE WHEN I GOT INTO YOUR ARMS;
THROUGH THIS STARS I CAN FEEL THE GLITTERING IN MY EYES WHEN I LOOK UPTO YOU;
ALL REMIND ME OF YOURS.
THOUGH YOU ARE NOT FAR FROM ME,
BUT AT THIS LONELY NIGHT AND SO MANY QUERIES IN MY MIND
IT SEEMS LIKE YOU ARE MILES AWAY FROM ME.
BUT YOU KNOW WELL THAT OUR HEARTS ARE CONNECTED

SOON THIS LONELINESS WILL CONVERT INTO HAPPINESS.
BY KEEPING ALL THE PROBLEMS BESIDE
WE'LL ENJOY SUCH NIGHT BELOW THE BLANQUET OF STARS
AND LOVE WE FEEL IN THE ARMS OF EACH OTHER.
ONLY ME,YOU AND SUCH ROMANTIC NIGHT
WITH THE HAPPINESS IN CLOCK NINE.
ON THAT DAY,I'LL FIND MY PEACE,MY HAPPINESS,MY LIFE
WHICH ALL EXIST WITH YOU.
THE LOVE WHICH I WAS SEARCHING FOR DAY AND NIGHT
AND I FOUND THAT ON THE LAP OF MINE.
I WANT TO HOLD THAT NIGHT FOREVER JUST LIKE YOU
I WISH THE TIME STOPS THERE AND ALL I CAN FEEL WAS YOU
ON THAT NIGHT,I NEED NOT TO FIND YOU IN THE BEAUTY OF IT.
RATHER, WE WE WILL ENJOY IT'S BEAUTY TOGETHER
HOLDING EACH OTHER'S HAND ON WINDY NIGHT.
- ISHA KHANDELWAL
(WAITING FOR THAT NIGHT EGARLY,<3)

Chapter7

THE GIRL WHO USED TO BE AFRAID OF THE DARK,

NOW FINDS PEACE IN IT.

SHE IS NOW LIKE A ROOM FULL OF DARKNESS.

SHE FINDS THE DARKNESS OF THE ROOM IN HER SOUL

THE SILENCE BUT LOUD SCREAM IN HER HEART

THE CALM AND PEACE LOOK JUST AS THE DARK ROOM.

SHE WANTS TO SEE THE STARS,

BUT IT'S JUST THE DARKNESS ATTRACTS HER SOUL

ONE DAY SHE WILL PUT DARKNESS IN HER HAND

WHICH WILL POINT OUT THE STARS TOO.

SHE FELL INTO DARKNESS

UNDER MANY THOUGHTS SHE HAD GONE

SHE IS NOW BECOMING STRONG

I AM NOW BECOMING STRONG.

THE SUN SETS AND RISE AGAIN

BUT I FEEL LIKE I WON'T RISE AGAIN.

I AM NOW A COMPLETE DARK ROOM

AND I HOPE TO BE A ROOM FULL OF LIGHT SOON.

I AM BROKE

SO HOW COULD YOU FIND ME AS A WHOLE.
LET ME BE IN PAIN
OTHERWISE HOW WILL I WRITE
IF I FIND HAPPINESS AGAIN?
MY LIPS ARE SEALED AND IMPRISONED BY THIS
SILENCE
THE NIGHT IS EVEN DARKER THAN USUAL
BUT THIS TOO SHALL PASS
I STILL HAVE SOME BELIEF
THAT THE DAY WILL BE BRIGHTER AGAIN
THE ROOM WILL BE LIGHTEN UP AGAIN
AND I'LL BE HAPPY AGAIN.
~ISHA KHANDELWAL

Chapter8

I WAS SOMEWHERE ON THE COASTLINE,
WASHED UP ON THE SHORE
WITH SALTWATER RATTLING IN MY LUNGS
AND SEAWEED TANGLED IN MY HAIR.
MY DIARY GOT WASHED AWAY
IN THE FLOW OF WATER
I HAVE LOST IT
JUST LIKE I LOST YOU.
EVERY ROMANTIC SONG REMINDS ME OF YOU,
EVERY ROMANTIC MOVIE I IMAGINE WATCHING
IS WITH YOU,
I WAS A FREE VERSE BUT YOU LIKE SONNETS
MORE,
I WAS WAITING FOR YOU
BUT YOU LEFT ME ALL ALONE.
OUR SOUL TOUCHED EACH OTHER
MY LOVE SPEAKS TO YOURS;
YOUR LOVE WARMS MY COLD HEART
MY ENDING WORLD WAS RESTARTING
YOU MADE IRRELEVANT RELEVANT
YOU MADE ME BRAVE;
BUT AS SOON AS I WANTED TO HOLD YOU
AND SAY THAT YOU ARE MINE.

YOU PUSHED ME AWAY
AND I FELT LIKE I WAS DYING.
AND NOW MY MIND IS FREEZED
I DON'T KNOW WHAT TO WRITE.
JUST LIKE MY INCOMPLETE STORY
THIS PEICE IS ALSO INCOMPLETE
I AM LIVING WITHOUT YOU,WITH A DYING HEART
SO HOW COULD THIS BE COMPLETE?
AND I AM LIVING THIS AS A BROKEN ART.
~ISHA KHANDELWAL

Chapter9

MOM!YOUR GIRL IS GROWN UP

AND SHE WANNA LET YOU KNOW A LOT MORE THINGS.

THE FAVOURIATE DISHES OF HER,ISN'T HER FAVOURIATE ANYMORE

THE SHOW FROM WHICH SHE COULDN'T TAKE HER EYES OFF

IS NOW THE SHOW WHICH MAKES HER TIRE EVEN MORE.

MOM!YOUR GIRL IS LIKE AN EMPTY VESSEL

AND THE NOICES ARE BEING PRODUCED IN HER HEART.

SHE WANNA LET YOU KNOW EVERY UPS AND DOWNS OF HER LIFE

BUT THERE IS SOMETHING WHICH IS STOPPING HER NOW.

MOM! I WANNA FLY, I WANNA EXPLORE THE SKY

BUT I DON'T WANT ANYONE TO CUT MY WINGS OR TO PREY.

MOM, I AM NOT THAT STRONG

BUT I WAN'T TO MAKE YOU FEEL PROUD.

I WANNA PAY THE DEBT OF EVERY SINGLE TEARS OF YOURS.

I KNOW I DON'T EXPRESS MY LOVE FOR YOU
BUT TRUST ME MY LOVE FOR YOU IS IMMORTAL.
I DON'T CRY IN FRONT OF YOU FOR MY PROBLEMS
BUT I WANT THE TIGHTEST HUG FROM YOU.
I AM SO TIRED OF THIS WORLD.
I WANNA LAY IN YOUR ARMS FORVER.
I KNOW YOU ARE ALSO A NORMAL HUMAN
YOU ALSO GET SAD.
YOU ALSO BREAK DOWN EVERY SINGLE DAY.
YOU ALSO WANT TO EXPLORE THE WORLD.
BUT EVEN AFTER ALL THIS YOU WORK FOR US.
I WANNA ADOPT THOSE STRENGTH AND BOLDNESS FROM YOU
YOU HAVE PACKED YOURSELF IN A CLOSED ROOM FOR ME,FOR US
AND YOU HAVE SACRIFICED EVERYTHING.
AND I AM SORRY THAT I DON'T DESERVE A BIT OF IT
SOMETMES I JUST WANNA HOLD YOUR HAND AND SLEEP LIKE A KID.
MY HEART FEELS SO RELAXED SEEING TO SLEEP QUIETLY
THAT I JUST WANNA STARE YOU THE WHOLE NIGHT.
YOU ARE THE BEST THNG FOR ME NO MATTER HOW MUCH I FIGHT WITH YOU.

SORRY FOR HIDING THINGS FROM YOU
DESPITE OF KNOWING THAT YOU KNOW ME
NINE MONTHS BEFORE THIS WORLD DO.
SORRY FOR SHOUTIG AT YOU SOMETIMES EVEN IF
YOU COME TO PAMPER ME.
SORRY FOR HIDING THIS LETTER TOO, WHICH I
DON'T KNOW WHEN YOU WILL SEE.
~YOUR HEART

Chapter 10

IT'S A BEAUTIFUL NIGHT AND LEAVES ARE FALLING DOWN FROM TREES.
I AM LOST SOMEWHERE IN THIS SOOTHING BREEZE.
I THINK I AM LOST IN YOUR DREAMS
AND I DON'T KNOW WHAT IS SEEMS?
THINKING ABOUT YOU DAY AND NIGHT
IS THE REASON I LOST MY SMILE.
I KNOW THAT HOW DO I SURVIVE
IT'S SEVEN MONTHS LONG WE HAVEN'T TALKED
BUT STILL THOSE THOUGHTS COME S TO MY MIND.
REVINDING THOSE MEMORY GIVES ME A SMILE
BUT I THINK THAT SMILE ALSO FLEW AWAY WITH THAT FIGHY.
JUST ONE CLICK TO THE GALLARY AND ALL THE MEMORIES REVIND
BUT THE TRARS ROLLING DOWN FROM MY EYES,
MAKES ME WEAK FROM INSIDE.
NOW I AM HAPPY ENOUGH IN MY LIFE
AND I DON'T THINK THAT I AM GONNA CRY.
A NEW DAY, A NEW BEGINNING
WITH A HAPPY SMILE AND GROWING HEART.

~ISHA KHANDELWAL.

So yes this was my very first attempt to write this. i appologize for my mistakes. more books on the way Ijust wanna explore every single thing i am interested in. hope you like it.